THE BOOK OF BENEDICTIONS

The Lord spoke to Moses, saying, "Speak to Aaron and his sons, saying, Thus you shall bless the people of Israel: you shall say to them,

> *The Lord bless you and keep you;*
> *the Lord make his face to shine upon you and be gracious to you;*
> *the Lord lift up his countenance upon you and give you peace."*

"So shall they put my name upon the people of Israel, and I will bless them."

Numbers 6:22-27

THE BOOK OF BENEDICTIONS

A Collection of Blessings from the Holy Bible, English Standard Version

With the monograph *The Lord's Supper*

Adrian V W Freer

wcp

Welford Court Press

The Book of Benedictions: A Collection of Blessings from the Holy Bible, English Standard Version. With the monograph *The Lord's Supper*

Welford Court Press
4 Whitebeam Road
Oadby
Leicester LE2 4EA
United Kingdom
www.webdatauk.wixsite.com/welford-court-press

First Edition 2013, revised 2016, 2022

British Library Cataloguing-in-Publication Data
A catalogue record for this book is available from the British Library.

ISBN: 978-09520304-6-1

ASIN: B00E5BIGH4

Cover image: St Peter's Parish Church, Gaulby, Leicestershire, England.

CONTENTS

Illustrations 6
Acknowledgements 7
Dedication 8
Preface 9

1 About benedictions 11
2 Preaching God's word 13
3 Old Testament benedictions 24
4 New Testament benedictions 26
5 Supplementary benedictions 35
6 Benediction subject themes 38
7 Closing hymns 40
8 The Lord's Supper 60
  The early years (AD 30 – AD 300)
  The dark years (AD 400 – AD 1500)
  The dawn breaks through (AD 1500 – AD 1571)
  Archbishop Laud (1620-1643)
  The scene in 1985

Appendices
I Bibliography 88
 Copyright notice 88
II The author 89
III Author's doctrinal statement 91
Index 94
Books by Adrian V W Freer 96

ILLUSTRATIONS

Rev Ashley Cheesman 8
Three-decker pulpit at Kings Norton church 13
St Peter's Church, Gaulby 15
St John the Baptist Church, King's Norton 16
Stained glass window at Gaulby church 18
St Michael & All Angels Church, Illston-on-the-Hill 19
Church of St Clement or St John, Little Stretton 21
Stained glass window at Illston-on-the-Hill church 23
Queen Mary I of England otherwise known as Bloody Mary 61
The Ascension 63
Mosaic depicting the Emperor Constantine I 64
The Pope as the Antichrist, signing and selling indulgences 65
Massacre of the Waldensians of Mérindol 66
Martin Luther before the Diet of Worms, 1521 68
Archbishop Thomas Cranmer 69
Hugh Latimer and Nicholas Ridley martyred at Oxford 70
Martyrdom of Thomas Cranmer in 1556 71
Queen Elizabeth I of England 72
Archbishop William Laud 74
Canterbury Cathedral 75
Roman Catholic stone altar with cross and two monstrances 77
St Peter's Church, Gaulby 78
The Last Supper, embossed copper picture 79
Protestant communion table 82
Jesus breaking bread in the upper room 83
Bishop John Hooper 84
The author 89

[Images are by the author unless otherwise stated]

ACKNOWLEDGEMENTS

The author would like to record his appreciation to the following people and organizations who have assisted in the preparation of this book.

I am indebted to the family of the late Ashley F B Cheesman for kindly granting permission to publish the monograph entitled *The Lord's Supper,* written by him. Thanks are given to Jana Hall who has agreed to the reproduction of the image of Rev Ashley Cheesman. I would also like to express my appreciation to Helen Ives for checking and verifying the tunes that accompany the hymns and for making many helpful suggestions. The words of the hymns are collated from a number of hymn books that are now in the public domain.

It is also very appropriate to acknowledge my gratitude to Wikipedia for making so many historic pictures in the public domain available under the Wikimedia Commons licence and such images are identified in the text.

Scripture quotations are from The Holy Bible, English Standard Version® (ESV®), copyright © 2001 by Crossway, a publishing ministry of Good News Publishers. Used by permission. All rights reserved. Where indicated the English Standard Version Anglicised (ESVUK®) has been used in order to conform to everyday United Kingdom English spelling.

Extracts from *The Book of Common Prayer*, the rights of which are vested in the Crown, are reproduced by permission of the Crown's Patentee, Cambridge University Press.

Finally, I would like to record my sincere thanks to my wife, Louise, for her encouragement with my literary efforts, for reading the numerous proofs and re-proofs, and for making many valuable suggestions.

DEDICATION

This book is dedicated to the memory of the late Rev Ashley F B Cheesman (1953-2010), rector of the Parish of Gaulby, Leicestershire, England from 1988 until his untimely death in 2010. During his ministry at Gaulby Parish, Rev Cheesman oversaw the work at St Peter's Church, Gaulby; St John the Baptist Church, King's Norton; St Michael & All Angels Church, Illston-on-the-Hill; and the Parish Church of St Clement or St John, Little Stretton.

Rev Ashley Cheesman
Image: courtesy of Jana Hall

The monograph entitled *The Lord's Supper*, written around 1985 by Rev Cheesman, is reproduced at the end of this book as a fitting memorial to a humble, faithful and much loved pastor of his flock, and a loyal and diligent servant of the Lord Jesus Christ.

PREFACE

It would no doubt be appropriate at the outset to explain the reasons why this book was written. It came about as a result of the author's need to choose a suitable benediction to conclude church services and when taking prayers. Extempore and written prayers can be fine, but why settle for second best when the Bible, God's inspired and inerrant word, contains so many suitable passages which are helpful, comforting, encouraging and challenging.

To fulfil this need the author set about to compile a selection of suitable verses from the Bible which were assembled into a little booklet intended for personal use and which was used during sermon preparation and subsequently carried along with the sermon notes.

When looking for an appropriate benediction it was always a source of wonder that there was always something that was totally appropriate. That should not really come as any surprise, however, when God Himself is the ultimate author of all scripture!

Friends who also preached requested copies of the booklet and the feedback from them appeared positive. As a result it was decided to offer the book to a wider audience and further research expanded the number of verses which have been included in this present volume.

The benedictions may be used exactly as they are, or alternatively they can follow a short extempore prayer which is appropriate to the passage that has been expounded, as the speaker deems appropriate.

As an aside and an additional benefit, when we are suffering the trials and troubles of this life, or enduring the venomous assaults from the enemy of our souls, reading verses such as these can be a great comfort. The precious blessings and promises contained in God's word can, with the sustaining grace of the Holy Spirit, help us to re-double our efforts to remain faithful when the difficulties arise. It is often at such times that our lives demonstrate our love and total reliance upon our Saviour in a very evident manner and in so doing bring the glory to Him.

To conclude this book there is a selection of hymns that are appropriate for closing church services and this is followed by the monograph *The Lord's Supper* by Rev Ashley Cheesman which examines the contrasts between the simple, Protestant communion service of remembrance, and the idolatrous and superstitious 'sacrifice' of the Mass; tracing its history (and the history of the church) from the New Testament era until the present day

It is the author's sincere prayer that this book will not only help those who are entrusted with the solemn responsibility of preaching God's word as they seek to build up believers in their most holy faith and present the gospel to the unconverted; but also encourage them to utilize some of the perhaps lesser used benedictions. It is also hoped that it will be of help to all believers as they meet with God during their daily quiet time.

Adrian V W Freer

Leicester

Chapter 1

ABOUT BENEDICTIONS

A benediction is the proclamation of God's divine blessing upon His people which is customarily pronounced at the end of a church service, prayer meeting or other religious gathering.

The Zondervan Dictionary of Bible and Theology Words gives the following definition: *Benediction: A pronouncement of divine favour, usually conferred toward the end of a discourse or letter (see Hebrews 13:20-21). Webster's Dictionary* describes it with the following words: *Benediction: The short prayer which closes public worship; as, to give the benediction.* Finally, the *Holman Bible Dictionary* defines the word as follows: *Benediction: A prayer for God's blessing or an affirmation that God's blessing is at hand. The most famous is the priestly benediction (or Aaronic blessing) in Numbers 6:24-26.*

Benedictions are used to give glory to God and to encourage, comfort and motivate His people. Such blessings reassure Christians that God has promised never to leave them or forsake them (Hebrews 13:5) as they are dismissed and re-enter the wider world to be living witnesses to the saving power of Jesus Christ and an influence for good on those around them and society at large.

The vast majority are to be found in the New Testament although there are several very familiar ones in the Old Testament. The well-known benediction in Numbers, which God gave to Moses to pass on to Aaron and his sons to bless the people, is possibly the most widely used benediction of all.

Most of the writers of the New Testament epistles: Paul, Peter, John, Jude and the writer to the Hebrews used benedictions in their letters. They generally appear at the conclusion of their writings although some are to be found at the beginning and elsewhere throughout them as well. That being the case the use of benedictions is a totally scriptural pattern to follow and we must be grateful that there are so many recorded examples in the Bible.

The passages collected here have been reproduced exactly as they are recorded in the Bible, but a few may need to be amended very slightly to make them more appropriate but without changing the meaning in any way (see the penultimate paragraph of this chapter).

To conclude the benedictions there is a short selection of supplementary blessings taken from service books, hymn books and other sources which the reader might also wish to consider.

The English Standard Version® (ESV) has been used in this book but alternative translations may be utilized if that is felt to be more appropriate and it is a simple matter to look up other versions using the references quoted after the passages.

The wording of a few of the New Testament benedictions in chapter four may need to be omitted or amended slightly to make them appropriate when the blessing is given (for example when the original benediction contained a reference to a specific New Testament church) and where this is the case the relevant word(s) have been enclosed in [square brackets] with the symbol ‡ appended after the Bible reference.

In order to conform to everyday United Kingdom English spelling, the English Standard Version Anglicised Edition has been used in a few places and on such occasions the Bible reference has been appended ESVUK.

Chapter 2

PREACHING GOD'S WORD

The most important activity that takes place when the Lord's people meet together for worship is, without doubt, the preaching of God's word. In order that those listening obtain the greatest benefit such preaching should include a number of complementary facets. It should explain the attributes of our almighty God in order that His people can rightly worship Him, it needs to teach sound doctrine in order to build up believers in their most holy faith and so enable them to avoid the pitfalls of sin and live lives that are pleasing to God, and it must proclaim the gospel message of salvation. It is crucially important that these aspects are all regularly and faithfully proclaimed.

Sound, biblical preaching involves an in-depth exposition of the doctrines contained within the passage or subject being addressed and this should be followed by the application which logically derives from it. That is the established pattern in pretty well all the New Testament epistles with two notable exceptions: in Philippians they are mixed together and 1 Corinthians would seem to answer a series of questions.

Three-decker pulpit at Kings Norton church with pulpit, reading desk and lectern

PREACHING THE GOSPEL

Those who have been entrusted with the solemn responsibility of preaching the gospel of Jesus Christ (see James 3:1) have a serious message to proclaim. It tells of the sinful, fallen state of mankind which is spiritually dead in trespasses and sin, is at enmity with God, and who has no possibility whatever to redeem itself.

The truth of the matter is that fallen man is so far estranged from God that, unless he is spiritually revived by the Holy Spirit, he is totally unable to do anything whatever to redeem himself. He is as spiritually dead as a lifeless corpse upon a mortuary slab! The Bible tells us that without the regenerating work of the Holy Spirit the gospel is not only incomprehensible to man, *'For the word of the cross is folly to those who are perishing, but to us who are being saved it is the power of God'* (1 Corinthians 1:18); but also that it is an offence to him, *'but we preach Christ crucified, a stumbling block to Jews and folly to Gentiles'* (1 Corinthians 1:23).

The good news of the gospel, however, is that God, through His infinite goodness and mercy, has provided a lifeline through repentance and faith in the substitutionary, atoning sacrifice of His only Son, the sinless Jesus Christ, and His shed blood on the cross at Calvary. As a result, man can be reconciled to God and have Jesus' perfect righteousness imputed to his account. Such is God's unfathomable mercy towards sinful mankind that not only is salvation a free gift of grace; but the faith to believe is given as a free gift as well! What a glorious message Christians have to proclaim!

THERE IS ONLY ONE GOSPEL

There is only one gospel whereby sinners may be saved and all others are nothing but a deceptive error. The apostle Peter declared the truth that there is only one gospel that can save sinners in his sermon at Pentecost recorded in Acts 4:12, *"'And there is salvation in no one else, for there is no other name under heaven given among men by which we must be saved.'"* In a similar manner the apostle Paul told his readers in Galatia, '*But even if we or an angel from heaven should preach to you a gospel contrary to the one we preached to you, let him be accursed. As we have said before, so now I say again: If anyone is preaching to you a gospel contrary to the one you received, let him be*

St Peter's Church, Gaulby (1741)

accursed' (Galatians 1:8-9). These are very strong words. The misconception of what election truly entails has resulted in countless (but doubtless well-meaning) people trying to alter the gospel message to make it more 'appealing' and so endeavour to convert unbelievers.

Paul declared in 2 Corinthians 4:2-3, '*But we have renounced disgraceful, underhanded ways. We refuse to practice cunning or to tamper with God's word, but by the open statement of the truth we would commend ourselves to everyone's conscience in the sight of God. And even if our gospel is veiled, it is veiled to those*

15

who are perishing'. The apostle was not prepared to alter the gospel in any way and neither should preachers today.

In the light of that the only thing that preachers can do is to faithfully proclaim that one true gospel and leave the outcome

St John the Baptist Church, King's Norton (1760)

to God to sovereignly call those whom He has elected, from before the foundation of the world, to be a part of His kingdom. There is no way that those who preach the gospel have any part in the actual decision making process of who is, and who is not, brought to faith. Indeed, we do not know who the elect are and that is why the gospel has to be preached to every creature.

THE COST OF TRUE DISCIPLESHIP

Our Lord Jesus challenged those who professed that they would forsake all to follow Him to weigh up the cost before doing so in Luke 14:25-33 when He said, *"So therefore, any one of you who does not renounce all that he has cannot be my disciple"* (verse 33). Genuine Christianity is a truly life-changing transformation where we surrender absolutely everything to

16

become servants, indeed slaves, of Jesus Christ. Christianity is not something that is tacked on to our existing lifestyle which is carried on pretty much as before, but rather it is one where believers live completely transformed lives.

Christians have a joy in knowing Jesus Christ as their Lord and Saviour that is beyond that of those who do not know Him, but in what is probably the most challenging statement anywhere in His teaching, in Matthew 7:15-23, Jesus presents the litmus test for our Christian faith: does it display the necessary fruit? That fruit is not only a love for God but also a holy fear (Psalm 111:10, Luke 12:5) and obedience to His commands (John 14:15). To those who do not display this fruit Jesus has these crushing words in verses 21-23, '*"Not everyone who says to me, 'Lord, Lord,' will enter the kingdom of heaven, but the one who does the will of my Father who is in heaven. On that day many will say to me, 'Lord, Lord, did we not prophesy in your name, and cast out demons in your name, and do many mighty works in your name?' And then will I declare to them, 'I never knew you; depart from me, you workers of lawlessness."'* Genuine Christianity is a serious matter: in reality it is a matter of life and death. It is whether we have peace with God or are at enmity with Him in this present world, and whether we are destined for a glorious eternity in heaven to be with Him or bound for destruction.

True discipleship does have a very real price to pay – but to those who have truly understood the gospel message, and what Christ has saved them from, it is worth surrendering absolutely everything to gain Christ. The apostle Paul had this to say in Philippians 3:8, '*Indeed, I count everything as loss because of the surpassing worth of knowing Christ Jesus my Lord. For his sake I have suffered the loss of all things and count them as rubbish, in order that I may gain Christ*'.

Sadly, and all too predictably, as a result of not understanding the gospel message correctly many of those who are seemingly 'converted' do not last the course and fall away at the very first hurdle when the inevitable problems of life come along.

WORSHIP IS A SERIOUS MATTER

How we approach and worship God is a serious matter. The salutary episode recorded in Leviticus 10:1-7 of when Nadab and Abihu, Aaron's two eldest sons, were punished by death for offering unauthorized (or strange) fire, in a manner contrary to that prescribed by God, is a dire warning of the seriousness of the matter. We are not told the precise nature of this fire, and it is probably left unspecified as a warning that *all* unprescribed ways are unacceptable, but it is possible that they added something which the Lord had not commanded to the day's ritual. The warning that follows shortly afterwards, about consuming strong drink (verse 9), suggests that they could well have been influenced by alcohol at the time.

Stained glass window at Gaulby church with the ascension (upper) and empty tomb (lower)

In a similar manner, when Cain offered a sacrifice that was not acceptable to God it was rejected and the consequences were disastrous when Cain subsequently murdered his brother Abel (Genesis 4:1-16).

Our God is indeed a *'consuming fire'* (Hebrews 12:29)

NURTURING NEW CONVERTS

In their zeal to add new members to their fellowships it has not been unknown for churches to place insufficient emphasis on the vital responsibility of nurturing new converts in the faith and so enable them to develop spiritually.

If they are to grow as they should, new Christians need to be taught both the doctrines of the faith and also the way in which that doctrine affects how they live their daily lives after conversion. Once we have been saved from our sin the Bible tells us that we become new creations in Christ and are totally different people. In 2 Corinthians 5:17 the apostle Paul

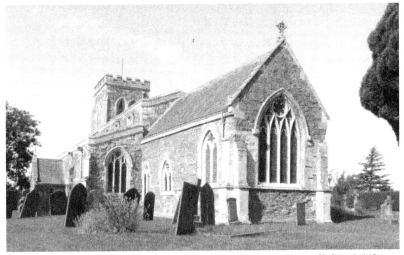

St Michael & All Angels Church, Illston-on-the-Hill (c.1250)

describes the transformation like this; *'Therefore, if anyone is in Christ, he is a new creation. The old has passed away; behold, the new has come.'*

The Bible uses the word 'sanctification' to describe the on-going process whereby Christians, both newly converted and those who have been believers for many years, grow and become more Christ-like on a day-by-day basis throughout the

19

rest of their earthly lives (see 2 Peter 3:18). We shall, of course, only be made completely perfect once we enter into the glory of heaven, but we do begin that process right now in this earthly life.

It is not only those who are new to the faith who need instruction; those who have been believers for many years need to be encouraged to continue and press on in their Christian pilgrimage through this mortal life until they meet with their Saviour.

CONTEMPORARY CHURCH

Ever since the formation of the early church, preaching the gospel has always been the means by which the great advances in the work of the church have progressed. At those times when the church has deviated from this path it has inevitably gone into decline until it has repented of its sin and turned back once more to God's ordained method.

That being the case it is disturbing to see that all too many pulpits in our land appear to have lost faith in the ability of God's Word to convert sinners. They mistakenly think that they know better than God and the method that He has ordained. Such foolish thinking not only shows a lack of faith; it is wilful disobedience and demonstrates what little confidence such people have in the power of God's word.

Many churches, in their attempt to be 'in tune with' and indistinguishable from the world, have side-lined expository preaching and in its place resorted to entertainment, drama, contemporary music and even such things as puppets, mime and other devices in their endeavours to 'reach' the lost. Not only that, some attempt to make their premises look as little like a church as possible and more like a social hall, coffee shop or sports arena. In past generations believers took great pains to ensure that the churches they erected were distinct from other buildings and possessed an ambiance that encouraged solemnity, reverence and enabled folk to experience the presence of God in a very real way (witness the four beautiful churches under Rev Cheesman's care portrayed in this chapter). That is why folk spoke in such places in whispered, guarded tones. Sadly that seriousness and solemnity is lacking in all too many of our churches today.

Church of St Clement or St John, Little Stretton (c. 1180)

As such churches have changed, so has the vocabulary that is used within them. 'Offensive' words such as sin, wrath, condemnation, hell and repentance appear to have all but vanished. The holy God of the Bible, who is not only a God of love, but is also a God of wrath who will judge the wicked for their sin, is replaced by one who is your 'chum' and who will meet your perceived needs with health, wealth and prosperity. Such a gospel places undue focus on God's love and that He will save you, which is undoubtedly true, but precisely from what and why He will save you is not always clearly spelled out. The Bible makes it quite plain that God is angry with sinners every single day, *'God is a righteous judge, and a God who feels*

21

indignation every day' (Psalm 7:11) and that facet of His character is all too often side-lined.

THE SITUATION TODAY

It is disturbing to see how the Western nations, once at the forefront in the proclamation of the reformed Protestant faith, have declined in both morality and godliness in recent decades and the responsibility for this decay must firmly be laid at the foot of the church, both established and non-conformist, as they have capitulated to secular ideas. The Bible is very clear in its instructions as to how society should operate and the way that individuals should live their daily lives, those commands being for our good and not to restrict us in any way. Nevertheless the church has willingly gone along with, and indeed actively promoted, many of the ungodly agendas promoted by unbelievers which are in direct opposition to God's laws: downgrading of the Lord's Day, gender identity, family life, homosexuality, abortion, evolution – the list is sadly a long one.

In times past the vast body of the British statute book was very firmly based upon biblical precepts but sadly that is no longer the case and as the years have passed the laws of our land have deviated ever further from God's wise commands. The results of this wilful disobedience are plainly evident in every aspect of modern society.

As a result the church has not become more popular as it might perhaps have hoped, but rather it is seen as weak, confused, irrelevant and very often an object of derision. In addition, as the God-fearing generations have passed away, they have been replaced by lukewarm churchgoers who see church as little more than a periphery activity and the consequences of professing allegiance to Christ as a price they are unwilling to pay. They would certainly not go to the stake for their faith as did the Protestant martyrs of old.

Thankfully there is still a godly remnant in the church, God always preserves a small band of loyal followers who remain faithful to Him, regularly attend church and loyally serve their Lord and Saviour for many decades, but such folk are under increasing pressure from both within and without the professing church.

Such a serious situation must surely drive every true believer to their knees to pray. Firstly, that God in His sovereign grace and mercy would bring revival to our church and nation rather than judge and punish us as we rightly deserve; and secondly, that those who are called to preach will be faithful to the one, true and only gospel which can save sinners. By doing things in God's appointed way we can pray confidently that the proclamation of His word will be blessed by Him and that the Holy Spirit will use the humble efforts of men to achieve His purposes and turn cold hearts to God.

Stained glass window at Illston-on-the-Hill church

23

Chapter 3

OLD TESTAMENT BENEDICTIONS

The Lord bless you and keep you; the Lord make his face to shine upon you and be gracious to you; the Lord lift up his countenance upon you and give you peace.

Numbers 6:24-26

Let your heart therefore be wholly true to the Lord our God, walking in his statutes and keeping his commandments.

1 Kings 8:61a

Lift up the light of your face upon us, O Lord!

Psalm 4:6b

May the Lord give strength to his people! May the Lord bless his people with peace!

Psalm 29:11

Blessed be the Lord forever! Amen and Amen.

Psalm 89:52

The Lord will keep you from all evil; he will keep your life. The Lord will keep your going out and your coming in from this time forth and forevermore.

Psalm 121:7-8

Those who trust in the Lord are like Mount Zion, which cannot be moved, but abides forever. As the mountains surround Jerusalem, so the Lord surrounds his people, from this time forth and forevermore.

Psalm 125:1-2

You keep him in perfect peace whose mind is stayed on you, because he trusts in you. Trust in the Lord forever, for the Lord God is an everlasting rock.

Isaiah 26:3-4

Chapter 4

NEW TESTAMENT BENEDICTIONS

And now I commend you to God and to the word of his grace, which is able to build you up and to give you the inheritance among all those who are sanctified.

Acts 20:32

To all those [in Rome] who are loved by God and called to be saints: Grace to you and peace from God our Father and the Lord Jesus Christ.

Romans 1:7 ‡

Oh, the depth of the riches and wisdom and knowledge of God! How unsearchable are his judgements and how inscrutable his ways! "For who has known the mind of the Lord, or who has been his counsellor?" "Or who has given a gift to him that he might be repaid?" For from him and through him and to him are all things. To him be glory for ever. Amen.

Romans 11:33-36 ESVUK

Do not be conformed to this world, but be transformed by the renewal of your mind, that by testing you may discern what is the will of God, what is good and acceptable and perfect.

Romans 12:2

May the God of endurance and encouragement grant you to live in such harmony with one another, in accord with Christ Jesus, that together you may with one voice glorify the God and Father of our Lord Jesus Christ.

Romans 15:5-6

May the God of hope fill you with all joy and peace in believing, so that by the power of the Holy Spirit you may abound in hope.

Romans 15:13

Now to him who is able to strengthen you according to [my] gospel and the preaching of Jesus Christ, according to the revelation of the mystery that was kept secret for long ages but has now been disclosed and through the prophetic writings has been made known to all nations, according to the command of the eternal God, to bring about the obedience of faith—to the only wise God be glory forevermore through Jesus Christ! Amen.

Romans 16:25-27 ‡

To the church of God [that is in Corinth], to those sanctified in Christ Jesus, called to be saints together with all those who in every place call upon the name of our Lord Jesus Christ, both their Lord and ours: Grace to you and peace from God our Father and the Lord Jesus Christ.

1 Corinthians 1:2-3 ‡

The grace of the Lord Jesus be with you.

1 Corinthians 16:23

Grace to you and peace from God our Father and the Lord Jesus Christ.

2 Corinthians 1:2

And God is able to make all grace abound to you, so that having all sufficiency in all things at all times, you may abound in every good work.

2 Corinthians 9:8

Finally, brothers, rejoice. Aim for restoration, comfort one another, agree with one another, live in peace; and the God of love and peace will be with you.

2 Corinthians 13:11

The grace of the Lord Jesus Christ and the love of God and the fellowship of the Holy Spirit be with you all.

2 Corinthians 13:14

Grace to you and peace from God our Father and the Lord Jesus Christ, who gave himself for our sins to deliver us from the present evil age, according to the will of our God and Father, to whom be the glory forever and ever. Amen.

Galatians 1:3-5

The grace of our Lord Jesus Christ be with your spirit, brothers. Amen.

Galatians 6:18

Grace to you and peace from God our Father and the Lord Jesus Christ.

Ephesians 1:2

[that] the God of our Lord Jesus Christ, the Father of glory, may give you the Spirit of wisdom and of revelation in the knowledge of him, having the eyes of your hearts enlightened, that you may know what is the hope to which he has called you, what are the riches of his glorious inheritance in the saints, and what is the immeasurable greatness of his power toward us who believe, according to the working of his great might that he worked in Christ when he raised him from the dead and seated him at his right hand in the heavenly places, far above all rule and authority and power and dominion, and above

every name that is named, not only in this age but also in the one to come.

Ephesians 1:17-21 ‡

Now to him who is able to do far more abundantly than all that we ask or think, according to the power at work within us, to him be glory in the church and in Christ Jesus throughout all generations, forever and ever. Amen.

Ephesians 3:20-21

Peace be to the brothers, and love with faith, from God the Father and the Lord Jesus Christ. Grace be with all who love our Lord Jesus Christ with love incorruptible.

Ephesians 6:23-24

Grace to you and peace from God our Father and the Lord Jesus Christ.

Philippians 1:2

[And] it is my prayer that your love may abound more and more, with knowledge and all discernment, so that you may approve what is excellent, and so be pure and blameless for the day of Christ, filled with the fruit of righteousness that comes through Jesus Christ, to the glory and praise of God.

Philippians 1:9-11 ‡

And the peace of God, which surpasses all understanding, will guard your hearts and your minds in Christ Jesus.

Philippians 4:7

And the peace of God, which surpasses all understanding, will guard your hearts and your minds in Christ Jesus. Finally, brothers, whatever is true, whatever is honourable, whatever is just, whatever is pure, whatever is lovely, whatever is commendable, if there is any excellence, if there is anything worthy of praise, think about these things. [What you have learned and received and heard and seen in me—practise these things,] and the God of peace will be with you.

Philippians 4:7-9 ‡

[And my] God will supply every need of yours according to his riches in glory in Christ Jesus. To our God and Father be glory forever and ever. Amen.

Philippians 4:19-20 ‡

The grace of the Lord Jesus Christ be with your spirit.

Philippians 4:23

To the saints and faithful brothers in Christ [at Colossae]: Grace to you and peace from God our Father.

Colossians 1:2 ‡

Put on then, as God's chosen ones, holy and beloved, compassionate hearts, kindness, humility, meekness, and patience, bearing with one another and, if one has a complaint against another, forgiving each other; as the Lord has forgiven you, so you also must forgive. And above all these put on love, which binds everything together in perfect harmony. And let the peace of Christ rule in your hearts, to which indeed you were called in one body. And be thankful. Let the word of Christ dwell in you richly, teaching and admonishing one another in all wisdom, singing psalms and hymns and spiritual songs, with thankfulness in your hearts to God. And whatever you do, in word or deed, do everything in the name of the Lord Jesus, giving thanks to God the Father through him.

Colossians 3:12-17

Now may our God and Father himself, and our Lord Jesus, [direct our way to you, and may the Lord] make you increase and abound in love for one another and for all, as we do for you, so that he may establish your hearts blameless in holiness before our God and Father, at the coming of our Lord Jesus with all his saints.

1 Thessalonians 3:11-13 ‡

Now may the God of peace himself sanctify you completely, and may your whole spirit and soul and body be kept blameless at the coming of our Lord Jesus Christ. He who calls you is faithful; he will surely do it.

1 Thessalonians 5:23-24

The grace of our Lord Jesus Christ be with you.

1 Thessalonians 5:28

Grace to you and peace from God our Father and the Lord Jesus Christ.

2 Thessalonians 1:2

Now may our Lord Jesus Christ himself, and God our Father, who loved us and gave us eternal comfort and good hope through grace, comfort your hearts and establish them in every good work and word.

2 Thessalonians 2:16-17

Now may the Lord of peace himself give you peace at all times in every way. The Lord be with you all.

2 Thessalonians 3:16

The grace of our Lord Jesus Christ be with you all.

2 Thessalonians 3:18

To the King of ages, immortal, invisible, the only God, be honour and glory for ever and ever. Amen.

1 Timothy 1:17 ESVUK

The Lord be with your spirit. Grace be with you.

2 Timothy 4:22

[All who are with me send greetings to you.] Greet those who love us in the faith. Grace be with you all.

Titus 3:15 ‡

Grace to you and peace from God our Father and the Lord Jesus Christ.

Philemon 3

The grace of the Lord Jesus Christ be with your spirit.

Philemon 25

Now may the God of peace who brought again from the dead our Lord Jesus, the great shepherd of the sheep, by the blood of the eternal covenant, equip you with everything good that you may do his will, working in us that which is pleasing in his sight, through Jesus Christ, to whom be glory forever and ever. Amen.

Hebrews 13:20-21

Grace be with all of you.

Hebrews 13:25

May grace and peace be multiplied to you.

1 Peter 1:2b

Blessed be the God and Father of our Lord Jesus Christ! According to his great mercy, he has caused us to be born again to a living hope through the resurrection of Jesus Christ from the dead, to an inheritance that is imperishable, undefiled, and unfading, kept in heaven for you, who by God's power are being guarded through faith for a salvation ready to be revealed in the last time.

1 Peter 1:3-5

Greet one another with the kiss of love. Peace to all of you who are in Christ.

I Peter 5:14

To those who have obtained a faith of equal standing with ours by the righteousness of our God and Saviour Jesus Christ: May grace and peace be multiplied to you in the knowledge of God and of Jesus our Lord.

2 Peter 1:1b-2 ESVUK

[But] grow in the grace and knowledge of our Lord and Saviour Jesus Christ. To him be the glory both now and to the day of eternity. Amen.

2 Peter 3:18 ESVUK ‡

And we know that the Son of God has come and has given us understanding, so that we may know him who is true; and we are in him who is true, in his Son Jesus Christ. He is the true God and eternal life. Little children, keep yourselves from idols.

1 John 5:20-21

Grace, mercy, and peace will be with us, from God the Father and from Jesus Christ the Father's Son, in truth and love.

2 John 3

Peace be to you. The friends greet you. Greet the friends, each by name.

3 John 15

But you, beloved, building yourselves up in your most holy faith and praying in the Holy Spirit, keep yourselves in the love of God, waiting for the mercy of our Lord Jesus Christ that leads to eternal life.

Jude 20-21

Now to him who is able to keep you from stumbling and to present you blameless before the presence of his glory with great joy, to the only God, our Saviour, through Jesus Christ our Lord, be glory, majesty, dominion, and authority, before all time and now and for ever. Amen.

Jude 24-25 ESVUK

The grace of the Lord Jesus be with all. Amen.

Revelation 22:21

Chapter 5

SUPPLEMENTARY BENEDICTIONS

Grant, we beseech Thee, Almighty God, that the words, which we have heard this day with our outward ears, may through Thy grace be so grafted inwardly in our hearts, that they may bring forth in us the fruit of good living, to the honour and praise of Thy name; through Jesus Christ our Lord. Amen.

Book of Common Prayer

O Almighty Lord, and everlasting God, vouchsafe, we beseech Thee, to direct, sanctify and govern, both our hearts and bodies, in the ways of Thy laws, and in the works of Thy commandments; that through Thy most mighty protection, both here and ever, we may be preserved in body and soul; through our Lord and Saviour Jesus Christ. Amen.

Book of Common Prayer

The peace of God, which passes all understanding, keep your hearts and minds in the knowledge and love of God, and of His Son Jesus Christ our Lord; and the blessing of God Almighty, the Father, the Son and the Holy Ghost, be amongst you and remain with you always. Amen.

Book of Common Prayer

Prevent us O Lord, in all our doings with Thy most gracious favour, and further us with Thy continual help; that in all our works begun, continued, and ended in Thee, we may glorify Thy holy Name, and finally by Thy mercy obtain everlasting life; through Jesus Christ our Lord. Amen

Book of Common Prayer

Almighty God, who hast given us grace at this time with one accord to make our common supplications unto Thee; and dost promise that when two or three are gathered together in Thy Name thou wilt grant their requests: Fulfil now, O Lord, the desires and petitions of Thy servants, as may be most expedient for them; granting us in this world knowledge of Thy truth, and in the world to come life everlasting. Amen.

Book of Common Prayer

Be with us Lord, as we go out into the world. May the lips that have sung Your praise always speak the truth; may the ears which have heard Your Word listen only to what is good and may our lives as well as our worship be always pleasing in Your sight, for the glory of Jesus Christ our Lord. Amen.

The Father, whose glory fills the heavens, cleanse you by His holiness; Christ, who ascended to the heights, pour upon you the riches of His grace; and the Holy Spirit, the Comforter, equip and strengthen you. Amen.

The blessing of God Almighty, the Father, the Son and the Holy Spirit, be among you and remain with you always. Amen.

Eternal God and Heavenly Father, You have graciously accepted us as living members of Your Son our Saviour Jesus Christ. Send us now into the world in peace, and grant us strength and courage to love and serve You with gladness and singleness of heart; through Christ our Lord. Amen.

Go in peace in the power of the Spirit to live and work to God's praise and glory. Amen.

Praise God, from whom all blessings flow; praise Him, all creatures here below; praise Him above, ye heavenly host; praise Father, Son, and Holy Ghost.

Thomas Ken (1637-1711)

Lord, keep us safe this night, secure from all our fears; may angels guard us while we sleep, till morning light appears.

John Leland (1754-1841)

May the grace of Christ our Saviour, and the Father's boundless love, with the Holy Spirit's favour, rest upon us from above. Thus may we abide in union with each other and the Lord; and possess in sweet communion joys which earth cannot afford.

John Newton (1725-1807)

Chapter 6

BENEDICTION SUBJECT THEMES

Whilst all the benedictions reproduced here are eminently suitable to end any church service, some are perhaps more appropriate when specific subjects have been addressed. It is therefore hoped that the following (but by no means exhaustive) list of subject headings, with some appropriate benedictions for each one, will prove helpful.

Some of the benedictions have been listed under more than one category.

Blessing:
Numbers 6:24-26
Psalm 4:6b
Psalm 29:11
Philippians 4:23
2 Thessalonians 3:16

(The) Christian life:
1 Kings 8:61a
Psalm 89:52
Psalm 121:7-8
Psalm 125:1-2
Acts 20:32
Romans 12:2
Philippians 4:7-9
Colossians 3:12-17
1 Thessalonians 3:11-13
1 Thessalonians 5:23-24
Hebrews 13:20-21

(The) Church of Christ:
Romans 15:5-6
1 Corinthians 1:2-3
Ephesians 3:20-21
Philippians 1:9-11
3 John 15

Endurance:
Psalm 125:1-2
Romans 12:2
Romans 15:5-6
Jude 20-21

Future hope:
Ephesians 1:17-21
1 Thessalonians 3:11-13
1 Thessalonians 5:23-24
1 Peter 1:3-5
Jude 20-21

God:
Psalm 89:52
Romans 11:33-36
Romans 16:25-27
Ephesians 3:20-21
1 Timothy 1:17
1 Peter 1:3-5
Jude 24-25

Grace:
2 Corinthians 1:2
2 Corinthians 13:14
Philippians 4:23
Philemon 25
2 Peter 3:18
Revelation 22:21

Love:
Romans 15:5-6
Ephesians 6:23-24
Philippians 1:9-11
Colossians 3:12-17
1 Thessalonians 3:11-13

Peace:
Psalm 29:11
Isaiah 26:3-4
Romans 15:13
Galatians 1:3-5
Ephesians 6:23-24
Philippians 4:7
1 Thessalonians 5:23-24
2 Thessalonians 3:16
Philemon 3

Preservation:
Psalm 29:11
Psalm 121:7-8
Psalm 125:1-2
Galatians 1:3-5

(The) Scriptures
Acts 20:32
Romans 16:25-27
Ephesians 1:17-21
Colossians 3:12-17

Chapter 7

CLOSING HYMNS

It is very appropriate that, as God's people prepare to disperse and head for home after gathering for worship, they ask for His divine protection from accident and danger as they travel, and intreat Him to grant them a peaceful night's rest before they awaken to re-enter the secular world.

There are a number of beautiful, old hymns that were specifically written to close church services which express this sentiment and a selection is appended in this chapter. It is hoped that they will prove helpful when leaders come to consider the choice of an appropriate closing hymn.

The Reformers surely had this necessity very much in mind when they penned the words of *The Third Collect, for Aid against all Perils* in The Order for Evening Prayer set out in the 1662 *Book of Common Prayer* which reads as follows:

> *Lighten our darkness, we beseech thee, O Lord; and by thy great mercy defend us from all perils and dangers of this night; for the love of thy only Son, our Saviour, Jesus Christ. Amen.*

Such hymns and prayers demonstrate the absolute confidence that God's people can have in their Saviour to protect and preserve them at all times. Believers have the wonderful promises in God's word that *'In peace I will both lie down and sleep; for you alone, O Lord, make me dwell in safety'* (Psalm 4:8); and that whilst they are sleeping our God is fully awake at all times to sovereignly guard and watch over His beloved, *'Behold, he who keeps Israel will neither slumber nor sleep'* (Psalm 121:4).

Abide with me; fast falls the eventide   Tune: Eventide

1 Abide with me; fast falls the eventide;
The darkness deepens; Lord with me abide.
When other helpers fail and comforts flee,
Help of the helpless, O abide with me.

2 Swift to its close ebbs out life's little day;
Earth's joys grow dim; its glories pass away;
Change and decay in all around I see;
O Thou who changest not, abide with me.

3 I need Thy presence every passing hour.
What but Thy grace can foil the tempter's power?
Who, like Thyself, my guide and stay can be?
Through cloud and sunshine, Lord, abide with me.

4 I fear no foe, with Thee at hand to bless;
Ills have no weight, and tears no bitterness.
Where is death's sting? Where, grave, thy victory?
I triumph still, if Thou abide with me.

5 Hold Thou Thy cross before my closing eyes;
Shine through the gloom and point me to the skies.
Heaven's morning breaks, and earth's vain shadows flee;
In life, in death, O Lord, abide with me.

Henry Francis Lyte (1793-1847)
Copyright: Public Domain

All praise to Thee, my God, this night   Tune: Tallis Canon

1 All praise to Thee, my God, this night,
For all the blessings of the light;
Keep me, O keep me, King of kings,
Beneath Thine own almighty wings.

2 Forgive me, Lord, for Thy dear Son,
The ill that I this day have done,
That with the world, myself, and Thee,
I, ere I sleep, at peace may be.

3 Teach me to live, that I may dread
The grave as little as my bed;
Teach me to die, that so I may
Rise glorious at the awful day.

4 O may my soul on Thee repose,
And with sweet sleep mine eyelids close;
Sleep that may me more vigorous make
To serve my God when I awake.

5 Praise God, from whom all blessings flow;
Praise Him, all creatures here below;
Praise Him above, ye heavenly host;
Praise Father, Son, and Holy Ghost.

Amen.

Thomas Ken (1637-1711)
Copyright: Public Domain

Day is dying in the west   Tune: Sherwin

1 Day is dying in the west,
Heaven is touching earth with rest;
Wait and worship while the night
Sets her evening lamps alight
Through all the sky.

> *Holy, holy, holy, Lord God of Hosts!*
> *Heaven and earth are full of Thee!*
> *Heaven and earth are praising Thee,*
> *O Lord Most High!*

2 Lord of life, beneath the dome
Of the universe, Thy home,
Gather us, who seek Thy face,
To the fold of Thy embrace,
For Thou art nigh. (Refrain)

3 While the deepening shadows fall,
Heart of Love, enfolding all,
Through the glory and the grace
Of the stars that veil Thy face,
Our hearts ascend. (Refrain)

4 When forever from our sight
Pass the stars, the day, the night,
Lord of angels, on our eyes
Let eternal morning rise,
And shadows end. (Refrain)

Amen.

Mary Artemisia Lathbury (1841-1913)
Copyright: Public Domain

Ere I sleep, for every favour

Tune: Thanet

1 Ere I sleep, for every favour
This day showed
By my God,
I will bless my Saviour.

2 O my Lord, what shall I render
To Thy Name,
Still the same,
Gracious, good, and tender?

3 Leave me not, but ever love me;
Let Thy peace
Be my bliss,
Till Thou hence remove me.

Amen.

John Cennick (1718-1755)
Copyright: Public Domain

Father, in high heaven dwelling

Tune: Evening Hymn (Jackson)

1 Father, in high heaven dwelling,
May our evening song be telling
Of Thy mercy large and free.
Through the day Thy love has fed us,
Through the day Thy care has led us
With divinest charity.

2 This day's sins, O pardon, Saviour,
Evil thoughts, perverse behaviour,
Envy, pride, and vanity;
From the world, the flesh, deliver,
Save us now, and save us ever,
O Thou Lamb of Calvary!

3 From enticements of the devil,
From the might of spirits evil,
Be our shield and panoply;
Let Thy power this night defend us,
And a heavenly peace attend us,
And angelic company.

4 Whilst the night-dews are distilling,
Holy Ghost each heart be filling
With Thine own serenity;
Softly let the eyes be closing,
Loving souls on Thee reposing,
Ever blessed Trinity.

George Rawson (1807-1889)
Copyright: Public Domain

God the Father! Be Thou near   Tune: Redhead 47

1 God the Father! Be Thou near,
Save from every harm tonight;
Make us all Thy children dear,
In the darkness be our light.

2 God the Saviour! Be our peace,
Put away our sins tonight;
Speak the word of full release,
Turn our darkness into light.

3 Holy Spirit! Deign to come!
Sanctify us all tonight;
In our hearts prepare Thy home,
Turn our darkness into light.

4 Holy Trinity! Be nigh!
Mystery of love adored,
Help to live, and help to die,
Lighten all our darkness, Lord!

George Rawson (1807-1889)
Copyright: Public Domain

46

Lord, dismiss us with Thy blessing   Tune: Dismissal

1 Lord, dismiss us with Thy blessing,
Thanks for mercies past receive;
Pardon all, their faults confessing;
Time that's lost may all retrieve;
May Thy children
Ne'er again Thy Spirit grieve.

2 Bless Thou all our days of leisure;
Help us selfish lures to flee;
Sanctify our every pleasure;
Pure and blameless may it be;
May our gladness
Draw us evermore to Thee.

3 By Thy kindly influence cherish
All the good we here have gained;
May all taint of evil perish
By Thy mightier power restrained;
Seek we ever
Knowledge pure and love unfeigned.

4 Let Thy father-hand be shielding
All who here shall meet no more;
May their seed-time past be yielding
Year by year a richer store;
Those returning,
Make more faithful than before.

John Fawcett (1740-1817)

My Father, for another night   Tune: St Timothy

1 My Father, for another night
Of quiet sleep and rest,
For all the joy of morning light,
Thy holy name be blest.

2 Now with the new-born day I give
Myself anew to Thee,
That as Thou willest I may live,
And what Thou willest be.

3 Whate'er I do, things great or small,
Whate'er I speak or frame,
Thy glory may I seek in all,
Do all in Jesus' name.

4 My Father, for His sake, I pray,
Thy child accept and bless;
And lead me by Thy grace today
In paths of righteousness.

Henry Williams Baker (1821-1877)
Copyright: Public Domain

New every morning is the love

Tune: Melcombe

1 New every morning is the love
Our wakening and uprising prove;
Through sleep and darkness safely brought,
Restored to life and power and thought.

2 New mercies, each returning day,
Hover around us while we pray;
New perils past, new sins forgiven,
New thoughts of God, new hopes of heaven.

3 If on our daily course our mind
Be set to hallow all we find,
New treasures still, of countless price,
God will provide for sacrifice.

4 The trivial round, the common task,
Will furnish all we need to ask,
Room to deny ourselves, a road
To bring us daily nearer God.

5 Only, O Lord, in Thy dear love
Fit us for perfect rest above;
And help us, this and every day,
To live more nearly as we pray.

John Keble (1792-1866)
Copyright: Public Domain

Now the day is over

Tune: Eudoxia

1 Now the day is over,
Night is drawing nigh;
Shadows of the evening
Steal across the sky.

2 Jesus, give the weary
Calm and sweet repose;
With Thy tend'rest blessing
May my eyelids close.

3 Comfort ev'ry suff'rer
Watching late in pain;
Those who plan some evil,
From their sin restrain.

4 Thro' the long night-watches
May Thine angels spread
Their bright wings above me,
Watching round my bed.

5 When the morning wakens,
Then may I arise
Pure and fresh and sinless
In Thy holy eyes.

Sabine Baring-Gould (1834-1924)
Copyright: Public Domain

Once more, before we part   Tune: Dennis

1 Once more, before we part,
Oh, bless the Saviour's name!
Let every tongue and every heart
Adore and praise the same.

2 Lord, in Thy grace we came,
That blessing still impart;
We met in Jesus' sacred name,
In Jesus' name we part.

3 Still on Thy holy word
Help us to feed, and grow,
Still to go on to know the Lord,
And practice what we know.

4 Now, Lord, before we part,
Help us to bless Thy name;
Let every tongue and every heart
Adore and praise the same.

Joseph Hart (1712-1768)
and Robert Hawker (1753-1827)
Copyright: Public Domain

Saviour, again to Thy dear name we raise   Tune: Ellers

1 Saviour, again to Thy dear name we raise
With one accord our parting hymn of praise.
Once more we bless Thee ere our worship cease,
Then, lowly bending, wait Thy word of peace.

2 Grant us Thy peace upon our homeward way;
With Thee began, with Thee shall end, the day;
Guard Thou the lips from sin, the hearts from shame,
That in this house have called upon Thy name.

3 Grant us Thy peace, Lord, through the coming night;
Turn Thou for us its darkness into light.
From harm and danger keep Thy children free,
For dark and light are both alike to Thee.

4 Grant us Thy peace throughout our earthly life,
Our balm in sorrow and our stay in strife;
Then, when Thy voice shall bid our conflict cease,
Call us, O Lord, to Thine eternal peace.

John Ellerton (1826-1893)
Copyright: Public Domain

Saviour, now the day is ending

Tune: Gounod

1 Saviour, now the day is ending,
Once again on Thee we call.
Let Thy Holy Dove, descending,
Bring Thy mercy to us all;
Set Thy seal on every heart;
Jesus, bless us ere we part!

2 Bless the gospel message spoken
In Thine own appointed way;
Give each longing soul a token
Of Thy tender love today;
Set Thy seal on every heart;
Jesus, bless us ere we part!

3 Comfort those in pain or sorrow;
Watch each anxious child of Thine;
Grant us hope for each tomorrow,
Strengthened by Thy grace divine;
Set Thy seal on every heart;
Jesus, bless us ere we part!

4 Pardon Thou each deed unholy;
Lord, forgive each sinful thought;
Make us contrite, pure, and lowly,
By Thy great example taught;
Set Thy seal on every heart;
Jesus, bless us ere we part!

Amen.

Sarah Doudney (1841-1926)

The day is past and over

Tune: St Anatolius

1 The day is past and over;
All thanks, O Lord, to Thee,
I pray Thee now that sinless
The hours of dark may be;
O Jesu, keep me in Thy sight,
And guard me through the coming night.

2 The joys of day are over;
I lift my heart to Thee,
And ask Thee that offenceless
The hours of dark may be;
O Jesu, keep me in thy sight,
And guard me through the coming night.

3 The toils of day are over;
I raise the hymn to Thee,
And ask that free from peril
The hours of dark may be;
O Jesu, keep me in Thy sight,
And guard me through the coming night.

4 Be Thou my soul's preserver,
For Thou alone dost know
How many are the perils
Through which I have to go;
O loving Jesu, hear my call,
And guard and save me from them all.

Greek 6th cent.
tr. by John Mason Neale (1818-1866)
Copyright: Public Domain

The day Thou gavest, Lord, is ended   Tune: St Clement

1 The day Thou gavest, Lord, is ended,
The darkness falls at Thy behest;
To Thee our morning hymns ascended,
Thy praise shall sanctify our rest.

2. We thank thee that Thy Church, unsleeping
While earth rolls onward into light,
Through all the world her watch is keeping
And rests not now by day nor night.

3. As o'er each continent and island
The dawn leads on another day,
The voice of prayer is never silent,
Nor dies the strain of praise away.

4. The sun that bids us rest is waking
Our brethren 'neath the western sky,
And hour by hour fresh lips are making
Thy wondrous doings heard on high.

5. So be it, Lord; Thy throne shall never
Like earth's proud empires, pass away;
Thy kingdom stands, and grows for ever,
Till all Thy creatures own Thy sway.

John Ellerton (1826-1893)
Copyright: Public Domain

The radiant morn hath passed away   Tune: Radiant morn

1 The radiant morn hath passed away,
And spent too soon her golden store;
The shadows of departing day
Creep on once more.

2 Our life is but a fading dawn,
Its glorious noon how quickly past
Lead us, O Christ, when all is gone,
Safe home at last.

3 O by Thy soul-inspiring grace
Uplift our hearts to realms on high
Help us to look to that bright place
Beyond the sky,

4 Where light, and life, and joy, and peace,
In undivided empire reign,
And thronging angels never cease
Their deathless strain;

5 Where saints are clothed in spotless white,
And evening shadows never fall;
Where Thou, Eternal Light of Light,
Art Lord of all.

Godfrey Thring (1823-1903)
Copyright: Public Domain

The sun is sinking fast

Tune: Twilight

1 The sun is sinking fast,
The daylight dies;
Let love awake, and pay
Her evening sacrifice.

2 As Christ upon the Cross
His head inclined,
And to His Father's hands
His parting soul resigned,

3 So now herself my soul
Would wholly give
Into His sacred charge
In whom all spirits live;

4 Thus would I live: yet now
Not I, but He
In all His power and love
Henceforth alive in me:

5 One sacred Trinity,
One Lord Divine;
Myself for ever His,
And He for ever mine.

Anonymous c.18th cent.
tr. by Edward Caswall (1814-1878)
Copyright: Public Domain

Thro' the day Thy love hath spared us

Tune: Through the day

1 Thro' the day Thy love hath spared us,
Now we lay us down to rest:
Thro' the silent watches guard us,
Let no foe our peace molest.
Jesus, Thou our Guardian be;
Sweet it is to trust in Thee.

2 Pilgrims here on earth and strangers,
Dwelling in the midst of foes,
Us and ours preserve from dangers;
In Thine arms may we repose
And, when life's short day is past,
Rest with Thee in heav'n at last.

Amen.

Thomas Kelly (1769-1854)
Copyright: Public Domain

We rest on Thee, our shield and our defender!

Tune: Finlandia

1 We rest on Thee, our Shield and our Defender!
We go not forth alone against the foe;
Strong in Thy strength, safe in Thy keeping tender,
We rest on Thee, and in Thy name we go;
Strong in Thy strength, safe in Thy keeping tender,
We rest on Thee, and in Thy name we go.

2 Yea, in Thy name, O Captain of salvation!
In Thy dear name, all other names above:
Jesus our righteousness, our sure foundation,
Our Prince of glory and our King of love,
Jesus our righteousness, our sure foundation,
Our Prince of glory and our King of love.

3 We go in faith, our own great weakness feeling,
And needing more each day Thy grace to know:
Yet from our hearts a song of triumph pealing,
"We rest on Thee, and in Thy name we go";
Yet from our hearts a song of triumph pealing,
"We rest on Thee, and in Thy name we go."

4 We rest on Thee, our Shield and our Defender!
Thine is the battle, Thine shall be the praise;
When passing through the gates of pearly splendour,
Victors, we rest with Thee, through endless days;
When passing through the gates of pearly splendour,
Victors, we rest with Thee, through endless days.

Edith Gilling Cherry (1872-1897)
Copyright: Public Domain

Chapter 8

THE LORD'S SUPPER

A monograph by Rev Ashley F B Cheesman

Note: The illustrations, captions and footnotes have been added and did not form part of the original text.

INTRODUCTION

It is a sad fact that the Sacrament of the Lord's Supper has been at the centre of the fiercest of the controversies which the Church of England has known during the four hundred and fifty years of her independent life. From her birth until the present day the Church of England has faced the greatest threats to her unity on the central issues surrounding the Communion Service.

The Church of England's reformers were willing to give up their lives at the stake during Queen Mary's reign, rather than concede their reformed views concerning the sacrament. In the sixteenth century the opposing positions were clear and well defined. Widely different positions are held today in the Church of England, but the situation is complicated by the sense of vagueness and uncertainty which has evolved, as to the true Anglican doctrine. A further complication arises from the false charity which prevails and which fosters the tendency not to criticise others who hold strong views.

The central issue is now, and always has been, whether the consecrated bread and wine in the communion service remain exactly and precisely as they were before, or whether there is some change in them. Is there or is there not any sense in which the sacramental bread and wine become the body and blood of the Lord Jesus Christ?

Does it really matter? The answer is yes. It mattered to the martyrs of the Church of England in Queen Mary's reign, and it should matter to us. The issue does not end with the sacramental bread and wine. When false views concerning the sacrament are pressed to their logical conclusion, it is the essentials of the gospel itself which are at stake. We need to know exactly where we stand when it comes to the Sacrament of the Lord's Supper.

I believe that there is no change whatsoever in the consecrated bread and wine. I believe that there is no sense in which Jesus Christ is received through the sacramental elements. Jesus is received in the communion service, by his believing people: not through their

Queen Mary I of England otherwise known as Bloody Mary
Image: Public domain/Wikimedia Commons

mouths but through FAITH, not into their stomachs but into their souls. To feed on Jesus is to apply the benefits of his death to ourselves.

I now endeavour to show that this view is the biblical position, and that it is the true Church of England teaching on the Lord's Supper. We must first examine the history of the church. We must trace the history of the Communion Service as the Church evolved and proceeded on its journey through the centuries of time since the Lord ascended to heaven, leaving his people in the guidance of the Word and Spirit. Before returning to the diversities and complexities of our own day we must look at four particular stages in the development of the Church:

- The early years (AD 30 – AD 300)
- The dark years (AD 400 – AD 1500)
- The dawning years (AD 1500 – AD 1600)
- The clouded years of error (AD 1600 – AD 1640)

We focus our attention on the Church's teaching and understanding of the Lord's Supper in these four key stages in the Church's history.

THE EARLY YEARS: (AD 30 – AD 300)

If we would see the Church at its best, carrying on its master's commands and commission, faithful in witness, filled with His Spirit and blessed by Him, we need look no further than the book of the Acts of the Apostles. There we see true faith; living, active, loving, working, faithful faith. The first followers of Jesus, fresh with their master's saving message, and motivated by His vision of a perishing humanity, lived in expectation of His imminent return. They were diligent to live by all the commands of Jesus. *'Do this in remembrance of me'* – the words used by Jesus in His instituting of the Communion – Luke 22:19, was a command they rejoiced to obey, not from a spirit of fear but from a spirit of love.

It should always be remembered that these early Christians enjoyed none of the privileges of religious freedom that we tend to take for granted in England in the late twentieth century. They were hated, both by the Jewish authorities and the civil authorities – i.e. the Roman government. Christianity was not a 'tolerated' religion. The followers of Christ were sought out and fiercely persecuted and indeed were often called upon to give up their earthly lives for the faith of Jesus Christ. Consequently they met in secret, not in splendid church buildings, but instead in cellars and crypts and deserted places. Their communions were simple – simple acts of remembrance. They expected and indeed received God's blessing, but the blessing came simply through their obedience in participating, through the powerful illustration impressed upon the mind of what it means to be daily feeding on the heavenly Paschal Lamb. There was no 'magic' or 'mystery' involved. They attached no hidden significance to Jesus' words *"This is my body"* and *"this is my blood"*. They rightly took these words in their simple and obvious sense – 'this represents my body – my blood'. Early Christian worship was characterised by its simplicity and sincerity and by the absence of mystery and superstition. And the early church was blessed by God.

Despite the severest of persecution and in a world far slower than our own, the gospel had spread throughout the Roman world and beyond within a hundred years of the apostles. Far from being eradicated, the church was growing and at a greater rate than it has ever

The Ascension, painting by Benvenuto Tisi (1481-1559)
Image: Public domain/Wikimedia Commons

grown since. God was with His Church. Jesus had promised '*I will never leave you alone... I will send you another comforter and He will be with you always*'.

You may think the picture I have drawn of the early church is a very rosy one, and surely it was not quite that simple. Of course there were difficulties, there were errors – how could it be otherwise when God's people are weak and sinful with a tendency to err and stray from God's truth. Even amongst the twelve disciples, remember, one betrayed Christ, another openly denied Him, and most of the others deserted Him when He hung on the cross. Yes, even in the third century errors were creeping in, both in faith and practice and with the beginnings of unspiritual clergy, but in general the church was at its best during the first two hundred and fifty years. It was not until the beginning of the fourth century, firstly with the Act of Toleration (AD 313) and then as Christianity quickly became fashionable throughout the Roman Empire, that the errors became widespread as pagan ideas were imported into the church, chiefly as a result of Baptism, the Supper of the Lord, and the Ministerial Office.

THE DARK YEARS: (AD 400 – AD 1500)

Detail of mosaic depicting the Emperor Constantine I with a model of the city of Constantinople
Image: Public domain/Wikimedia Commons

When the Emperor Constantine identified himself with the Christian faith early in the fourth century, the whole face of the Christian church changed and many of the problems of our church today may be traced back to Constantine and the ensuing rush of the Roman Empire to enter the Christian Church. The Church was eager to accept the newcomers into their fellowship without clear evidence of individuals' change of heart from the established heathen religions to real living faith in the Lord Jesus Christ. The beginnings of an unspiritual clergy helped in its lack of resistance to the changes necessitated by accommodating the mass of new members. Within a few generations the church ceased to be the active body of Christ: it was transformed into a heathen religion, covered only with a thin veneer of Christianity. Its witness died out and it became (in stark contrast to its persecuted origins) a proud, arrogant organisation – a persecutor itself, of others. The evil of the established church of the Roman Empire continued to grow until it reached its zenith in the dark years between AD 900 and AD 1500.

By the end of the fourth century a subtle change had taken place with regard to baptism. The significance of the heathen initiation rites became apparent when applied to the sacrament of baptism. The sacrament of baptism came to be substituted for the spiritual experience of which it is the outward seal. By a 'secret mystery' the rite of baptism

Woodcut depicting the Pope as the Antichrist, signing and selling indulgences c.1521
Image: Public domain/Wikimedia Commons

was thought to confer spiritual grace. From this we see the origin of the false doctrine of Baptismal Regeneration which still persists today, even in parts of the Church of England.

Very soon changes took place with regard to the Lord's Supper. It too became charged with 'magical' significance. Instead of the blessing being in the obedience of participation and in the powerful illustration to the mind of the meaning of daily feeding spiritually on the heavenly Paschal Lamb, now the blessing was in the actual eating and drinking of the sacramental bread and wine.

Other changes, clearly traceable from their heathen influences within the church were in regard to ministerial office, the church buildings, idolatry, the church's calendar and in respect to the position of Saints in the church, especially the Virgin Mary.

By the tenth century, the established church had ceased to be the Church of Christ. She had sunk into a worldly and

Massacre of the Waldensians of Mérindol by Provençal and papal soldiers in 1545
Image: Public domain/Wikimedia Commons

powerful organisation, riddled with idolatry, superstition and immorality. The Pope, or Bishop of Rome, had usurped the place of Christ and claimed headship of the Church. The church had become an instrument of terror to anyone who questioned its disgusting perversions of the gospel. To its everlasting shame it set about the extermination of those isolated groups of biblical Christians who were, during those wilderness years, the true representatives of Christ on earth – one such sect being the Waldensians[1] in southern France and northern Italy. The court of the Holy Inquisition was set up in 1210 to enforce submission to Rome and all its detestable demands and practices.

The full doctrine of the Mass was formed and enforced in 1209. All were required to believe (on peril of death) that at the moment of consecration the sacramental bread and wine were changed into the very literal flesh and blood of Christ. The minister, already a mediator, now became a sacrificing 'priest' in the true Old Testament sense of the word. It was supposed that he could, by reciting the mystical Latin formula, recreate God in Christ upon what now came to be called an altar. He then proceeded to destroy God on the altar, offering a sacrifice for the sins of the living and the dead (those in purgatory). Not a shred of this blasphemy is founded on warrant from the Holy Scriptures, but rather, the doctrine is repugnant to the Word of God (see Article 31).

It is true that on the eve of the Reformation there were voices within the established church, calling for reforms both in doctrine and practice, there were moves to end the gross immorality which had long existed and there were designs to curb some of the most extravagant departures from doctrinal truth (e.g. indulgences). However, there were no moves to reform the doctrine of the Mass, and it is worth remembering that even today the Church of Rome insists that a change takes place in the sacramental bread and wine at the moment of elevation, and that Christ is received through the bread and wine.

It was against this dark background that the light of the glorious Reformation broke through in the first half of the sixteenth century.

THE DAWN BREAKS THROUGH (AD 1500 – AD 1571)

It must surely have been over many years that the Holy Spirit had been working in the minds and temperaments of the men He had chosen to be the instruments of His truth. However, the visible Reformation did not commence until Luther's immortal stand for the truth in 1517. He and those who followed him, developing and continuing the advance of reform, were God's appointed agents as surely as were the prophets of old to idolatrous Israel.

The new teaching was immediately denounced and condemned by Rome, and was attacked with as much ferocity as the old organ of terror could muster. However, the teaching which was, of course, not so much new as revived after having been buried for many centuries, quickly spread through Northern Europe including our own country. England was not the first country to embrace as a nation, a reformed religion.

The story of Henry VIII's divorce from Catherine of Aragon is well known and it was the primary reason for the English break with Rome. Cessation from Rome was not in itself the reformation of the Church of England, although it paved the way for it. During the last years of Henry's reign the new Church of England moved slowly towards Reformation. Henry VIII died at Greenwich in 1545 and during the next four years the Reformation firmly took hold of England. With the first English prayer books of 1549 and 1552 came the end of the Mass and a true doctrine of the Lord's Supper in its place. Thrust out with the Mass was the whole medieval medley of superstition and error which surrounded it. During the unhindered years of

Martin Luther before the Diet of Worms, 1521

Image: Public domain/Wikimedia Commons

Reformation in England (1548–1553) a dedicated body of men emerged who were to lay down the foundations of our reformed Protestant Church of England.

Under the leadership of Archbishop Cranmer the godly zeal for the truth of men like Bishop Hugh Latimer, Bishop Nicholas Ridley, Bishop John Hooper, Bishop Ferrar, Archdeacon Philpott, John Bradford, Rowland Taylor and John Rogers, impressed the reformed truth of the gospel on the minds of the men and women of England under their spiritual care and protection.

Archbishop Thomas Cranmer (1489-1556)
Image: Public domain/Wikimedia Commons

In 1549 Cranmer invited Martin Bucer, a German Protestant reformer, to Cambridge to teach theology and assist in the English reformation. It was during the years of Edward VI's reign that Cranmer worked on the first book of homilies. Especially to be noted is his homily on 'Justification by Faith'.

The reformation years came to an abrupt end in 1553 with the death of King Edward VI and the accession to the throne of his eldest sister Mary. Queen Mary, the daughter of a devout Roman Catholic, Catherine of Aragon, swiftly proceeded to do all in her power to extinguish the reformation in the English church. Cranmer and his best Bishops and clergymen, those with reformed views, were quickly imprisoned; the reformed English prayer book of 1552 was immediately withdrawn and replaced by the Mass. Papal authority and rule was quickly re-imposed. The infamous anti-reformists Bonner and Gardiner[2] were elevated to the primary sees of Canterbury and London, and there followed five years of the severest persecution of Christians that England has ever known.

The leading reformers and all those who held reformed views were ruthlessly hunted down. They were to renounce their reformed views, affirm the universal supremacy of the Pope, or Bishop of Rome, and the truth of the leading Roman doctrines. In the subsequent trials of the leading reformers, it was the doctrines concerning the Lord's Supper which in every case became the focal point of their persecution and condemnation. They were required to affirm that "in the sacrament of the altar the sacramental bread and wine became the literal flesh and blood of Christ", or that "the body and blood of Christ are present under the forms of bread and wine after consecration".

Hugh Latimer and Nicholas Ridley martyred at Oxford in 1555
Image: Public domain/Wikimedia Commons

Almost to a man, the leading English reformers refused at this time. Other humiliation they could bear, but that Christ's body and blood could be reproduced in the sacramental bread and wine, they would not admit. And so they were condemned to be burned.

One by one the champions of the Reformation were led out to be publicly burned: Bishop Hooper outside his own Cathedral in Gloucester. Rowland Taylor in his own parish of Hadleigh in Suffolk, Bishops Latimer and Ridley back-to-back in

Oxford where the majority of the martyrs died. The accounts of their martyrdom, though gruesome, are moving and awesome. They went to the stake, not struggling, not in terror, but with an eager joy to meet their Lord face to face. Did they die like criminals? Were they mocked and jeered? – only by a few of their tormentors! They were surrounded by crowds of people, praying for them and encouraging them. The men and women of England, the poor and ordinary, were with them and behind them. Nothing did so much to strengthen the reformed Church of England than the martyrdom of her leading reformers. As the flames engulfed the two Bishops, Latimer cried out to Ridley: *"This day we shall light such a candle in England as I trust shall never be put out"*. Under the persecution of Queen Mary the reformed faith continued to grow. Just as in the early

Martyrdom of Thomas Cranmer in 1556
Image: Public domain/Wikimedia Commons

Church of the second century the truth flourished and the church grew under the persecution of the Roman Empire, so it was again in England in the days of Mary Tudor.

Of all the leading reformers only Archbishop Cranmer weakened and recanted his reformed views, even on the Lord's Supper. But at the end God graciously enabled him to repent of his recantation and he died a true martyr of the Reformation denouncing the blasphemy of the Mass and its vile doctrine of Transubstantiation. The history is well known of how he held out his right hand in the flames crying *"this hand shall burn first"* – the hand that signed his false recantation – *"for it sinned"*.

71

The leading reformers were dead and the truth once again held down under a ruthless tyranny: but the Reformation was not dead and the position was again reversed. Elizabeth I, Mary's younger half-sister and daughter of Anne Boleyn, was a confirmed Protestant. She immediately re-established the independence of the Church of England and re-instated the reformed 1552 prayer book with a slight revision of 1559. In

Queen Elizabeth I of England (1533-1603)
Image: Public domain/Wikimedia Commons

1562 the 39 Articles of Religion were agreed upon by the Archbishops and Bishops of both provinces, and the whole clergy in a convocation held in London that year. As their inscription states, their purpose was 'for the avoiding of diversities of opinions and for the establishing of consent touching true religion'. The Articles gave official ecclesiastical and doctrinal standing to the Homilies, many of which had been drawn up earlier by Cranmer, Hooper and other reformers.

The Articles were again ratified by the clergy and assented to by Queen Elizabeth I as supreme Governor of the Church of England in 1571. Article 28 on the Lord's Supper states "Transubstantiation (or the change of the substance of bread and wine) in the Supper of the Lord cannot be proved by Holy Writ, but it is repugnant to the plain words of Scripture... The body of Christ is given, taken and eaten, in the Supper, only after an heavenly and spiritual manner. And the means whereby the body of Christ is received and eaten in the Supper is FAITH."

The forty five years of Elizabeth I's reign provided a continuity in which the reformed principles became established throughout England. The medieval mystery of the 'Mass' was replaced by the simple communion act of remembrance. The communion tables were brought down from their east wall positions and placed in the body of the church. The trappings of the Mass were also removed – the bizarre ornamentation and any elaborate ceremonial which might give rise to any of the old superstitions of the Mass. The communion tables stood bare without any hangings that might give the appearance of an altar. During the prayer of consecration the minister stood at the north side of the table so that his actions were clearly visible to the congregation, removing the mystery that surrounded the prayer when the minister stood with his back to the people. Neither was there to be now any lifting up of the sacraments or any manual acts. (It must be remembered that in the medieval rite it was at the moment of 'elevation' that the alleged change was supposed to take place in the bread and wine).

During the reign of Elizabeth I the Church of England was in soundly reformed and doctrinal position, but it was never free from the dangers of unprotestantizing influences. It must be stated that the Elizabethan church had shortcomings. Partly because of the Queen's jealousy of her power in respect to Bishops, and partly because of her conciliatory policy towards Roman Catholics in seeking to 'win them over', the reforming work was not carried forward as energetically as it might have been. Petty rules were invoked on main points of church order, paving the way towards the great dissention of the 1660s. When any church begins to uphold orthodoxy at the cost of spirituality, the way is prepared for spiritual decay and danger. Such was the case at the close of the sixteenth century. This is one reason for the extraordinary rise to power of William Laud, who we examine under the next heading.

ARCHBISHOP LAUD (1620-1643)

For forty years this man waged war on the reformed Protestant Church of England. He set out with one determined aim: to unprotestantize the Church of England. We must presume that he sincerely believed that his actions were for God's benefit and for the good of the Church of England: but there can be no doubt that he was, in reality, a traitor to the reformed Church of England, and a tyrant to those over whom he had authority.

Archbishop William Laud (1573-1645)
Image: Public domain/Wikimedia Commons

He was ordained by Bishop Young at Rochester in 1601, and it was during the next few years, whilst he was engaged in university work, that he first became known for his disaffection towards sound reformed teaching. In various sermons and lectures he sought to undermine important reformed truths and outraged his Protestant colleagues. On several occasions he was reprimanded by his superiors. However, he gained influential friends who were later to assist him in his extraordinary rise to power in the Church of England.

In 1616 he was appointed Dean of Gloucester Cathedral. It must be remembered that sixty-five years earlier John Hooper had been Bishop of Gloucester and it was under his teaching, with other reformers, that the communion tables had been brought down from the east wall, where they stood as 'altars', and set up in the midst of the choir. Just sixty years earlier, still in living memory, John Hooper had been burned at the stake, within sight of the Cathedral, for refusing to abandon his reformed views, especially those concerning the Lord's Supper.

Now, in 1616, William Laud insisted on replacing the communion table back against the east wall. Both the Bishop and the people were strongly opposed to this, knowing that it tended to bring back the papal notion of an 'altar', and encouraged the idea of a sacrifice, and a 'priest', and the Mass, into the Lord's Supper. Laud had his way.

Due to the persistence of his influential friends, he was made a Bishop in 1621 and from that time on his policies took on an ever-widening sphere of influence. He never lost a moment in advancing his cause. He encouraged and gathered around him a group of men with similar views. His doctrines found eager adherents among the unspiritual. He rose to become Archbishop of Canterbury in 1633. Now his power and influence reached its peak. He relentlessly and meticulously pursued his policy of unprotestantizing the Church of England. This he did in a variety of

Canterbury Cathedral
Image: Public domain/Wikimedia Commons

ways. Firstly, from his position as Archbishop – a position of great influence – he fostered and nurtured a spirit of disaffection for the Reformation among the easily led, and less spiritual members of the Church. Secondly, he advanced his own particular principles by every way open to him. By injunctions to the clergy, guide lines, recommendations and, not least, by his own powerful example he brought into the

Church a whole series of suspicious innovations – each one in itself a trifle, but seen as a whole, an undoubted attempt to change the plain Protestant religion of the Church of England. Not only were the communion tables removed permanently to the east wall, but they were also to be fenced in (Laud used the shallow pretence of avoiding irreverence with respect to dogs and being used as seats!). Laud advocated candles, crosses, ornamentation, hangings to drape the Lord's Table, anything which seemed to give the appearance and flavour of an 'altar'. Significantly, he sought also to give official sanction to the dangerous word 'altar' itself. He encouraged bowing to the table, bowing at the name of 'Jesus', bowing down to the consecrated bread and wine. He also encouraged the forbidden practice of retaining some of the consecrated bread and wine to be kept in the church to be worshipped!

Laud openly declared his belief that the consecrated bread and wine changed into Christ's body and blood. He raised what he was pleased to call the 'altar' into a position of unwarranted superiority over the pulpit saying: "the altar is the most important place for there is Christ's body whereas from the pulpit comes only his word".

Laud's third line of attack on the Church of England was by persecution. His disgraceful treatment of French and Walloon refugee congregations in London was a prelude to his attack on men of his own church. Puritans were persecuted and brought before the ecclesiastical Courts and the Star Chamber for the most minor infringements whilst those who turned the Communion Service into a semi Popish Mass were openly encouraged! During Laud's reign of terror, many of the Church of England's best men were silenced, either through imprisonment or exile: men like Richard Baxter and Edward Calumny. The preaching of the gospel was openly hindered or belittled. The word of God, scripturally supreme, was thrust into a position of inferiority to the sacraments.

Laud wormed his way into the confidence of a foolish monarch, King Charles I, and also became a political figure whose intervention helped precipitate the Civil War of 1643-48.

Laud was eventually imprisoned in 1641 and executed in 1645 for crimes against the Church and state. He did not receive good treatment and his punishment was over-harsh; but he cannot be called a martyr of the Church for he was not without guilt and his cause was false. No one ever did more harm to the Church of England than Archbishop Laud, not even Bonner or Gardiner or Queen Mary I. Laud died in 1645 when his sad history was concluded on Tower Hill, but his works lived on. The effects of his policies were far reaching. Many of our present problems in the Church of England find their origin in

Roman Catholic stone altar with cross and two monstrances[3]

the effects of the policies of William Laud. He was the father of the extreme Ritualist movement and through that, of the Tractarian Movement, and through that, of the extreme Anglo-Catholic Movement which has made such advances in our present day.

THE SCENE IN 1985

What of the Church of England today? Is it still reformed and Protestant – the church that Hooper and Ridley and the martyred reformers would wish to belong to? Does Latimer's

77

candle still burn in England? These are hard questions. And they demand a very hard and mixed answer.

The Church of England is under attack on all sides. Just as in the Middle Ages when the true followers of Christ suffered under the cruel repression and persecution of Rome, just as in the days of Mary Tudor, and as in the days of Archbishop Laud, so is the Church of England today under threat and in peril. The reformed Protestant Church of England is under attack from two principle directions: the extreme Anglo-Catholic Movement on the one hand, and the extreme liberal movement on the other. Between these two extremes the true reformed teaching of the Church of England, though squeezed and hindered, is still upheld.

St Peter's Church, Gaulby

One of the benefits of the Church of England has always been her broadness. There is room for those of varying degrees of churchmanship. However, the present situation is not a beneficial broadness, nor is it a tolerable one. The limits of the Church have been broken. On the one side there are men of authority and position in the Church, men of considerable influence who openly deny some of the essentials of the gospel, down-grading the Lord and His word, the Bible. On the other side there are those who effectively bury the gospel under the sacraments and a whole heap of superstition and idolatrous innovations. Never more so than now did the Church of England need to mark our Lord's warning in Matthew 16 verses 5-12: *"Take heed and beware the yeast* [doctrine/teaching] *of the Pharisees and Sadducees".* With His

78

clear insight into human weakness and tendency to sin, He knew that His Church would never be free from error. He knew that there would always be those who would seek to add to the gospel the things of men, and that there would always be those who would seek to subtract from the gospel some of its essential truths. The Jewish sects of the Pharisees and the Sadducees died out soon after the time of the apostles, but their spiritual successors have continued throughout the history of the Church. They are seen today in the extreme Anglo-Catholic

The Last Supper, embossed copper picture at St Mary & All Saints Church, Stoughton, Leicestershire

Movement on one hand and the followers of extreme liberal theology on the other. When these two combine they form one of the deadliest foes to the gospel. In the so-called Anglo-Catholic Movement we so often see a combination of Romish views of the Church and extreme liberal theology concerning the Bible!

Beyond doubt, the martyred reformers would wring their hands in horror if they were permitted to look on their church today. Wherever Latimer's candle still flickers, it does so in spite of the tendencies that have spread through the Church of England since the days of Archbishop Laud.

We concentrate our attention on the Service of Holy Communion as it is seen in the Church of England in the late twentieth century. The view is very diverse. Reflections are seen of every standpoint from that of the reformers to that of the Church of Rome. Error exists and it may be exposed. Those who love the truth and have a concern for God's people are right to denounce error in the Church when that error threatens the spiritual life of the Church itself. No doubt they will be labelled, "narrow", "uncharitable", "alarmists" and "opponents of unity"; but there comes a time when truth must not be suppressed for the sake of unity or what passes for peace. That time has come in the Church of England.

In many of our churches the Communion Service has ceased to be a fair representation of the biblical institution, and has ceased to be the service envisaged by the reformers. What are the symptoms of these errors and by what standards may they be judged error according to the Church of England's teaching formularies?

Error exists wherever men and women believe the blessing of receiving communion to be in the actual act of eating and drinking the sacramental elements, rather than in the simple obedience to Christ's command and in the powerful illustration to the mind of feeding on Christ which the Lord's Supper provides. There is no lack of men of authority in the Church who seek to encourage this subtle but deadly change in emphasis. The following are the most obvious practices which encourage false notions:

1. The minister consecrates the bread and wine whilst standing in the position of a 'Sacrificing Priest', facing the table with his back to the people. (The practice is not allowed by the rubric of the *Book of Common Prayer*).

2. The minister lifts the bread and wine above his head at the moment of consecration. (A bell may be rung at this point). Historically, this is the moment when the bread and wine are supposed to change, (The practice is outlawed by Article 28).

3. The minister bows down to the consecrated elements. This gives the impression that a change has taken place in them. (This idolatrous practice is outlawed by Article 28 and by the note at the end of the Communion Service – *Book of Common Prayer*).
4. Some of the sacramental bread and wine is retained after the service – 'reserved'. It is placed in a box on the wall near the Lord's Table. A white light may burn above this box to signify the presence of the Sacrament. People are encouraged to kneel in front of this box as they pass, and to worship or adore its contents! (Outlawed by Article 28 – "The Sacrament of the Lord's Supper was not by Christ's ordinance reserved, carried about, lifted up or worshipped").
5. Suspicious innovations in the service, regrettably allowed in variations within the *Alternative Services Book* (1980) such as the 'Benedictus' and the 'Agnus Die' when they follow immediately after the prayer of consecration or during the administration. There is nothing suspicious in the wording, rather it is in their position after consecration. This gives credence to the notion of a change in the bread and wine. (Occasionally words such as "this is the Lamb of God" are used after consecration. This is not sanctioned even in the ASB).
6. The minister encourages a superstitious veneration of the Lord's Table. He calls it an 'altar' and bows before it. He encourages others to do the same. (The dangerous word 'altar' is carefully avoided in the *Book of Common Prayer*. Bowing to a table is idolatry).
7. Again, it is allowed in the ASB to accompany the distribution of the bread and wine with the plain words – 'the body of Christ' – 'the blood of Christ'. This tends towards the obvious error.

81

Behind these obvious tendencies towards the idea of a change in the bread and wine, there exists a whole range of apparent incidentals which serve to bolster the above practices. They are trifles; but pernicious trifles – the outward symptom of inward disease. Few churches are free from these phenomena – a result of the meticulous work of the Tractarian Movement in the last century. They often exist, even in evangelical churches, almost unnoticed: but they undoubtedly aid in the fostering of false doctrines and superstitious beliefs amongst the weak. The following are noted as the more important:

Protestant communion table

A. A 'sacred aura' is contrived to hang around the Lord's Table and the Chancel area. Candles may be placed on the table, incense may be burnt, and a metal cross may be placed thereon.

B. The Lord's Table itself is dressed up like a medieval 'altar': various hangings being draped around it.

C. An elaborate ceremonial in the Communion Service tends to heighten the idea of 'mystery'.

D. The minister wears a special dress for communion: an alb, chasuble or stole, which he would not wear for Matins or Evensong.

E. Wafers are substituted for ordinary bread in the Service. (This practice is disallowed in the *Book of Common Prayer*).

F. The sacrament is placed directly into the recipient's mouth, not into his hands. (This practice is also disallowed in the *Book of Common Prayer*).

G. The people turn towards the east – the direction of the Lord's Table – during the Creed. (This is an innovation which, like bowing at the mention of Jesus' name, was given credence by William Laud in the seventeenth century).

It is sad to have to consider all the points noted in these lists, but truth must be spoken. When we look at the simple institution of Jesus, and the teaching of the New Testament, and when we look at the history of the Church, it should be clear to the unbiased mind that these things tend toward a departure from essential truth. They tend toward the nurturing and the fostering of the superstitious belief that the sacramental bread and wine change in some way at consecration. When such beliefs are embraced, most of the leading truths of the gospel come under attack. The Lord's Supper is in danger of ceasing to be a sacrament – becoming a 'sacrifice' instead, so degrading our Lord's one, perfect, finished sacrifice at Calvary (See Article

Jesus breaking bread in the upper room, painting by Dieric Bouts (c.1420-1475)
Image: Public domain/Wikimedia Commons

31). Similarly, once grant that there are 'priests' who can offer sacrifices to God, the Priestly Office of Christ is spoilt, and He is robbed of His glory. The doctrine of the Christian ministry is also perverted when sinful men become mediators between God and man. A vile form of idolatry is produced when men and women give to the sacramental bread and wine an honour and veneration which they were never meant to be given. Again, once grant that the body and blood of Christ can be present in any way on our Lord's Table, (regardless of any clever use of words, e.g. 'spiritually present' or 'sacramentally present') the true doctrine of Christ's humanity is overthrown. If the body and blood of Christ could be present on the communion table, in any way – corporally, really, essentially, spiritually, or sacramentally – then His body could not be really human and He could never have been a true man. This is a denial of the true doctrine of the Manhood of Christ (See Article 2, and note at the end of the Communion, *Book of Common Prayer*).

Bishop John Hooper (1495-1555), Protestant reformer and martyr
Image: Public domain/Wikimedia Commons

When the significance of Jesus' words in John, chapter 6 – *"he who eats my flesh and drinks my blood has eternal life"* – is transferred to the sacramental bread and wine (the next progression of error), then the fundamental doctrine of Justification by Faith only is overthrown. Wrong views concerning the Lord's Supper and the sacramental bread and wine can easily lead to a complete denial of the gospel. Well did Bishop Hooper say of the doctrine of Transubstantiation in the sixteenth century, before he was burned at the stake … *"it is the darling of the devil, and the heir to Antichrist's religion"*. What of the true observance of the Lord's Supper? The true observance is as it commonly was in the first and second centuries AD, and as it was again at the Reformation in the doctrine and practice of the martyred reformers of the Church of England – a simple act of remembrance, with blessing expected and received through obedient participation and the vivid illustration to the mind of feeding on Christ which the Lord's Supper provides.

There is a right reverence and dignity in which the Service should be conducted and entered into. The highest blessings should be expected when we truly feed on Christ in our hearts by faith, and when we faithfully obey Christ's command – *"Do this in remembrance of me"*; but we are always inclined to seek after a more sensuous and showy religion. We must continually guard against false beliefs concerning the sacraments. We must check that our own observance is right, lest that which was ordained for our blessing should become our downfall and stumbling block.

The Church of England needs men and women with strong biblical convictions to stand up for the truth, to stand against error, and to fight for the reformed Protestant Church of England[4]. She is in troubled waters – many are in ignorance, many are in error. If she is to survive as a church worth preserving, those who love the truth must stand firm on the hard won ground of the Reformers.

May Latimer's candle continue to burn in England, and not be put out!

Footnotes:

1. The Waldensians were a sect of pre-Reformation Christians who rejected Roman Catholic practices contrary to the Bible (purgatory, indulgences, prayer for the dead, the veneration of saints, etc.; as well as the power, wealth and corruption of the papacy) which brought them into conflict with the Church of Rome. In contrast they adopted a simple lifestyle (they were known as 'the poor men of Lyons'), boldly preached the word of God, and most importantly held that the Communion Service was a memorial of Christ's death and not a sacrifice.

During the fifteenth century there was an interchange of ideas between the Bohemian Hussites, English Wyclifites who were to be found in central Europe, and the Waldensians; and there were sporadic attempts to unite the Hussites and Waldensians although these failed as a result of differences in doctrine.

When the Reformation began to spread the Waldensian synod held at Chanforan, Italy in 1532 decided to join the Reform Movement.

The following quotation provides a summary of their influence on church history: *'Nevertheless, such activity provided the charged atmosphere in which the great religious changes of the sixteenth century would occur, when many Waldensian beliefs entered the mainstream of the Protestant movement'* (*The History of Christianity,* page 317).

2. Edmund Bonner (c.1500–1569) and Stephen Gardiner (1483-1555) were two of the most vehement opponents of the Reformation in England and were responsible for the persecution (and deaths) of many of the Protestant reformers.

3. Monstrance: an open or transparent receptacle, very often in the form of a sunburst, used by the Roman Catholic Church to display the consecrated 'host' for veneration.

4. The errors of the Roman Catholic Church in respect of the Lord's Supper were such that four of the Thirty Nine Articles of the Church of England were written to refute their misinterpretation and they are reproduced below:

XXVIII. *Of the Lord's Supper.*

The Supper of the Lord is not only a sign of the love that Christians ought to have among themselves, one to another, but rather it is a sacrament of our redemption by Christ's death: insomuch that to such as rightly, worthily, and with faith receive the same, the bread which we break is a partaking of the body of Christ, and likewise the cup of blessing is a partaking of the blood of Christ.

Transubstantiation (or the change of the substance of bread and wine) in the Supper of the Lord, cannot be proved by Holy Writ, but is repugnant to the plain words of Scripture, overthroweth the nature of a Sacrament, and hath given occasion to many superstitions.

The body of Christ is given, taken, and eaten in the Supper, only after an heavenly and spiritual manner. And the mean whereby the body of Christ is received and eaten in the Supper is Faith.

The Sacrament of the Lord's Supper was not by Christ's ordinance reserved, carried about, lifted up, or worshipped.

86

XXIX. *Of the wicked which do not eat the body of Christ, in the use of the Lord's Supper.*

The wicked and such as be void of a lively faith, although they do carnally and visibly press with their teeth (as S. Augustine saith) the sacrament of the body and blood of Christ, yet in no wise are they partakers of Christ, but rather to their condemnation do eat and drink the sign or sacrament of so great a thing.

XXX. *Of Both Kinds.*

The Cup of the Lord is not to be denied to the lay people; for both parts of the Lord's sacrament, by Christ's ordinance and commandment, ought to be ministered to all Christian men alike.

XXXI. *Of the one oblation of Christ finished upon the Cross.*

The offering of Christ once made is the perfect redemption, propitiation, and satisfaction for all the sins of the whole world, both original and actual, and there is none other satisfaction for sin but that alone. Wherefore the sacrifices of Masses, in the which it was commonly said that the priests did offer Christ for the quick and the dead to have remission of pain or guilt, were blasphemous fables and dangerous deceits.

**St John the Baptist Church,
Kings Norton, Leicestershire**

Appendix I

BIBLIOGRAPHY

Blunt, D M. *Roman Catholicism: Christian or Counterfeit?* Christian Watch, Nuneaton, Warwickshire, 2010.

Cambridge University Press. *The Book of Common Prayer.* Cambridge University Press, Cambridge, 2004 edition.

Church Society. *The 39 Articles of Religion with an Introduction.* Church Society, Watford, Hertfordshire, 2012.

Cranmer, T, Jewel, J and others. *Sermons or Homilies Appointed to be Read in Churches.* Focus Christian Ministries Trust, Southampton, 1986.

Dowley, T (editor). *The History of Christianity.* Lion Publishing, Tring, Hertfordshire, 1977.

Foxe, J. *Fox's Book of Martyrs: A History of the Lives, Sufferings and Triumphant Deaths of the Early Christian and the Protestant Martyrs.* reprinted by Zondervan Publishing House, Grand Rapids, Michigan, USA, 1967.

Freer, A V W. *Quiet Time for Christians: A Practical Guide to Daily Bible Reading and Prayer.* Welford Court Press, Oadby, Leicestershire, 2017.

Lane, T. *The Lion Concise Book of Christian Thought.* Lion Publishing, Tring, Hertfordshire, 1984.

Packer, J I and Beckwith, R T. *The Thirty-Nine Articles: Their Place and Use Today.* Latimer House, Oxford, 1984.

COPYRIGHT NOTICE

Appendix II

THE AUTHOR

Adrian Freer was born and still lives in Leicestershire where he is now retired. He was educated at Loughborough Grammar School and Leicester College of Art & Technology (now De Montfort University).

He had a non-church upbringing and was a member of the Methodist Church before conversion.

After many years in the evangelical movement he settled under the ministry of the late Rev Ashley F B Cheesman, rector of the Parish of Gaulby, Leicestershire, England from 1988 until 2010.

The Gaulby Parish of Anglican churches was one of the Church of England parishes in the county of Leicestershire which upheld the doctrines of the English Reformers, subscribed to the Thirty Nine Articles of the Church of England and used the 1662 *Book of Common Prayer* in its services.

After the untimely death of Rev Cheesman in 2010 the work of the Gaulby Reformed Evangelical Anglican Fellowship continued for a further nine years until it finally closed in 2019.

Adrian Freer is the author of a number of books including *Burial or Cremation for Christians? A Biblical Pattern for Funerals* (EP Books), *Quiet Time for Christians: A Practical Guide to Daily Bible Reading and Prayer* (Welford Court Press) and *A Biblical Defence of the Sport of Angling: What the Bible Says About Fishing* (Welford Court Press).

Apart from church responsibilities, Adrian's other interests include fly fishing and fly tying, music, foreign travel and writing. He is married with two daughters and four grandchildren.

For further information visit Adrian Freer's website:
www.webdatauk.wixsite.com/adrian-freer

St Peter's Church,
Gaulby, Leicestershire

Appendix III

AUTHOR'S DOCTRINAL STATEMENT

Very often when reading religious books it is not always easy to ascertain the doctrinal position of the author at the outset. Although this will generally become clear as progress through the work is made, it would be useful to have this information beforehand.

All too often statements such as 'Bible Believing' and 'Christian' are made by those who clearly do not really believe that God's Word is inerrant and infallible in its entirety, have any real faith, or sometimes even believe in God.

The author suggests that it would be helpful if books contained a statement of the writer's doctrinal stance. That being the case the author has chosen to state his position here, and in the hope that other writers might do the same:

The author would describe himself as Protestant, evangelical in the 'traditional' meaning of the term, a five-point Calvinist[1], one who upholds the doctrines of the Reformers, and subscribes to the *Thirty Nine Articles of the Church of England* [with the reservation the Puritans had to Article XXVII concerning baptism].

With regard to controversies at the forefront at the present time: he believes (scripture teaches) a literal six day creation, the doctrine of election[2], marriage should *only* be between one man and one woman, church leadership and authority should be restricted to men, and he holds an a-millennial eschatological position[3].

With reference to the 'Israel' debate he understands that the church, comprising both believing Jews and Gentiles, is the fulfilment of the Old Testament nation of Israel (rather than the current geographical/political state of Israel).

Footnotes:

1. The book *TULIP: The Five Points of Calvinism in the Light of Scripture* by Duane Edward Spencer (Banner of Truth Trust, 1970) explains this issue.

2. The apostle Paul explained the doctrine of predestination and election in the following words, *'even as he chose us in him before the foundation of the world, that we should be holy and blameless before him. In love he predestined us for adoption to himself as sons through Jesus Christ, according to the purpose of his will'* (Ephesians 1:4-5).

In a similar manner, Article XVII of the Thirty Nine Articles of the Church of England states the following:

Article XVII *Of Predestination and Election.*

Predestination to life is the everlasting purpose of God, whereby, before the foundations of the world were laid, He hath constantly decreed by His counsel secret to us, to deliver from curse and damnation those whom He hath chosen in Christ out of mankind, and to bring them by Christ to everlasting salvation as vessels made to honour. Wherefore they which be endued with so excellent a benefit of God be called according to God's purpose by His Spirit working in due season; they through grace obey the calling; they be justified freely; they be made sons of God by adoption; they be made like the image of His only-begotten Son Jesus Christ; they walk religiously in good works; and at length by God's mercy they attain to everlasting felicity.

As the godly consideration of Predestination and our Election in Christ is full of sweet, pleasant, and unspeakable comfort to godly persons and such as feel in themselves the working of the Spirit of Christ, mortifying the works of the flesh and their earthly members and drawing up their mind to high and heavenly things, as well because it doth greatly establish and confirm their faith of eternal salvation to be enjoyed through Christ, as because it doth fervently kindle their love towards God: so for curious and carnal persons, lacking the Spirit of Christ, to have continually before their eyes the sentence of God's Predestination is a most dangerous downfall, whereby the devil doth thrust them either into desperation or into wretchlessness of most unclean living no less perilous than desperation.

Furthermore, we must receive God's promises in such wise as they be generally set forth to us in Holy Scripture; and in our doings that will of God is to be followed which we have expressly declared unto us in the word of God.

3. For a helpful exposition of this subject *The Momentous Event: A Discussion of Scripture Teaching on the Second Advent* by W J Grier (Baker Books, 1979) is well worth studying.

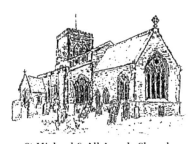

**St Michael & All Angels Church,
Illston-on-the-Hill, Leicestershire**

INDEX

Aaron 11, 18
Abel 18
Abihu 18
abortion 22
Act of Toleration 64
Acts of the Apostles 62
alcohol 18
altar 67, 74-76, 81-82
Anglo-Catholic Movement 77-79
Antichrist 65, 84
Archbishop of Canterbury 75
Articles of Religion 86-87, 92-93
ascension 18, 63

baptism 64, 65
Baptismal Regeneration 65
Boleyn, Anne 72
Bonner, Edmund 70, 77
Book of Common Prayer 68, 69, 72
Bucer, Martin 69

Cain 18
Catherine of Aragon 68, 69
Charles I, King 77
Cheesman, Rev Ashley 8, 60-85
church buildings 20-21
Church of England 60, 68-69,
    72-73, 77-78, 85
Civil War 77
communion table 73-76, 82
Constantine I, Emperor 64
Cranmer, Archbishop Thomas 69,
    71, 72

discipleship 16-18

Edward VI, King 69

elevation 67, 73
Elizabeth I, Queen 72-73
English Prayer Book – see *Book of
    Common Prayer*

family life 22
fear 17
fruit 17

Gardiner, Stephen 70, 77
gender identity 22
gospel 14-16, 63, 69

health, wealth and prosperity 21
Henry VIII, King 68
Holy Inquisition 66
homilies 69, 72
homosexuality 22
Hooper, Bishop John 69, 70, 72,
    74, 84
hymns 40-59

idolatry 66
indulgences 65, 67

Justification by Faith 69, 84

Latimer, Bishop Hugh 69-71
Latimer's candle 71, 77-78. 79, 85
Laud, Archbishop William 74-77
liberal movement 78, 79
Lord's Supper 60-87
love for God 17

magic 63, 65
martyrs 70-71, 84
Mary I, Queen 60-61, 69, 71
Mary Tudor – see Mary I, Queen

Mass 66-67
mediator 67, 83
Moses 11
mystery 63, 65, 73

Nadab 18
New Testament benedictions
    26-34

obedience 17, 63, 65, 80, 85
'offensive' words 21
Old Testament benedictions
    24-25

Paschal Lamb 63, 65
persecution 62-63, 65, 70-71, 76
Pharisees 78-79
Pope 65, 66, 70
preaching 13-14, 20
priest 67, 75, 83
pulpit 13, 76
purgatory 67
Puritans 76

quiet time 10

Reformation 67-73
remnant 23
revival 23
Ridley, Bishop Nicholas 69-71
Ritualist movement 77
Roman Catholics 73

Roman Empire 64, 71

Sadducees 78-79
Saints 66
sanctification 19-20
sleep 40
solemnity 21
stake 60, 71, 74, 84
Star Chamber 76
statute book 22
strange fire – see unauthorized
    fire
superstition 63, 66, 68, 78

Taylor, Rowland 69, 70
The Lord's Supper (monograph)
    60-85
Thirty Nine Articles of Religion
    72
Tractarian Movement 77, 82
Transubstantiation 72, 84

unauthorized fire 18

vestments 82
Virgin Mary 66

wafers 82
Waldensians 66, 85-86
worship 18, 63

TBOB11072022

**St Clement or St John Church,
Little Stretton, Leicestershire**

Quiet Time for Christians: A Practical Guide to Daily Bible Reading and Prayer

Adrian V W Freer

Setting aside a regular time each day to read God's Word and have a time of prayer is one of the most valuable disciplines for any Christian if they are to have a closer walk with their Saviour.

The aim of this book is twofold: firstly to assist those who already have a quiet time to make it more profitable and productive, and secondly to persuade those who do not as yet have a regular time alone with God to begin that rewarding and lifelong journey now.

Paperback: 158 pages, 54 illustrations, 6 tables and 1 map

Published by: Welford Court Press ISBN: 978-1798995303

Burial or Cremation for Christians? A Biblical Pattern for Funerals

Adrian V W Freer

In these days when cremation is so common, few realise that in Christian-influenced societies it originated only in the nineteenth century and that for many years the choice of burial or cremation was one primarily made on the grounds of the faith of the deceased and the relatives.

This book does not try to replay the debates of the past, but instead it takes a careful and balanced look at the biblical data and encourages thoughtful, prayerful planning. Helpful appendices contain suggested hymns and scriptures for funeral services.

Paperback: 108 pages, 29 Illustrations, 1 table and 1 map

Published by: EP Books ISBN: 978-1-78397-025

Printed in Great Britain
by Amazon

83045501R00058